D1607273

Helen Keller

Published in the United States of America by Cherry Lake Publishing
Ann Arbor, Michigan
www.cherrylakepublishing.com

Content Adviser: Ryan Emery Hughes, Doctoral Student, School of Education, University of Michigan
Reading Adviser: Marla Conn MS, Ed., Literacy specialist, Read-Ability, Inc.
Book Design: Jennifer Wahi
Illustrator: Jeff Bane

Photo Credits: © Carol M. Highsmith/Library of Congress, 5; © Bettmann/CORBIS, 7; © Everett Collection
Historical / Alamy Stock Photo, 9, 11; © Y is for Yellowhammer; illus. by Ted Burn, (Sleeping Bear Press), 13, 22;
photographer unknown, H100265 U.S. Copyright Office/Library of Congress, 15; © Whitman, Chelsea, Mass./
Library of Congress, 17, 23; © U.S. Embassy New Delhi/Flickr, 19; © Pictorial Press Ltd / Alamy Stock Photo, 21;
Cover, 12, 16, 18, Jeff Bane; Various frames throughout, Shutterstock Images

Library of Congress Cataloging-in-Publication Data

Names: Haldy, Emma E., author.
Title: Helen Keller / Emma E. Haldy.
Description: Ann Arbor, Michigan : Cherry Lake Publishing, 2016. | Series: My
    itty-bitty bio | Includes bibliographical references and index.
Identifiers: LCCN 2015045148| ISBN 9781634710206 (hardcover) | ISBN
    9781634712187 (pbk.) | ISBN 9781634711197 (pdf) | ISBN 9781634713177
    (ebook)
Subjects: LCSH: Keller, Helen, 1880-1968--Juvenile literature. | Deafblind
    women--United States--Biography--Juvenile literature. | Deafblind
    people--United States--Biography--Juvenile literature.
Classification: LCC HV1624.K4 H35 2016 | DDC 362.4/1092--dc23
LC record available at http://lccn.loc.gov/2015045148

Printed in the United States of America
Corporate Graphics

About the author: Emma E. Haldy is a former librarian and a proud Michigander. She lives with her husband, Joe, and an ever-growing collection of books.

About the illustrator: Jeff Bane and his two business partners own a studio along the American River in Folsom, California, home of the 1849 Gold Rush. When Jeff's not sketching or illustrating for clients, he's either swimming or kayaking in the river to relax.

my story

I was born in Alabama. It was 1880.

I got sick as a baby. I could not see. I could not hear.

4

Imagine you could not see or hear. What would that feel like?

I struggled to **communicate**.
I was angry.

I did not behave well. My family was upset.

I needed help. I visited doctors. They worked with the **deaf** and **blind**.

They said I should work with a teacher. They suggested Anne Sullivan.

Anne came to live with my family.
I was 6 years old.

Anne worked hard to teach me.
It was not easy at first. But Anne
found a way.

What would it be like to have your teacher live with you?

She helped me feel an object. Then she spelled the word in my hand.

The first word I learned was "water." It was a **miracle**!

13

I quickly made progress.
I learned to read **Braille**.
I learned to write. I even
learned to speak.

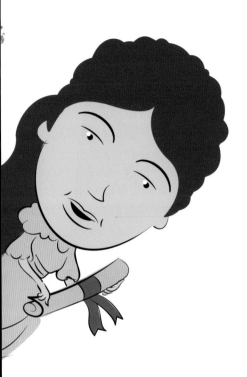

With Anne's help, I went to school. I graduated from college.

I wrote books. I traveled. I gave speeches.

I was a leader for deaf and blind people.

I started groups to help them.
I shared my story.

I won many awards. I was honored until my death at age 88.

I was a gifted woman. I was smart and **courageous**. I was a hero to my community.

What would you like to ask me?

1887

1870

↑ Born
1880

1904

1970

↑
Died
1968

glossary

blind (BLINDE) people who can't see

Braille (BRAYL) a system of writing and printing for blind people that uses raised dots for letters and numbers

communicate (kuh-MYOO-ni-kate) to share information, ideas, or feelings

courageous (kuh-RAY-juhs) able to do something scary

deaf (DEF) people who can't hear

miracle (MIR-uh-kuhl) a surprising and lucky event

index